COMPACT CYMRU

The C

A Journey from Tywyn to Bardsey

Photographs and Text

Jean Napier MA

Gwasg Carreg Gwalch

First published in 2022
© Jean Napier MA / Gwasg Carreg Gwalch

Published by Gwasg Carreg Gwalch,
12 Iard yr Orsaf, Llanrwst, Conwy, LL26 0EH.
tel: 01492 642031
email: llyfrau@carreg-gwalch.cymru
website: www.carreg-gwalch.cymru

ISBN: 978-1-84524-512-2

Cover photos: Jean Napier

Previous Books

Jean Napier MA
Bardsey – Now and Then
  ISBN 978-1-84524-287-9
Rhinogydd – Ancient Routes and Old Roads
  ISBN 978-1-84524-271-8
Rhosydd – A Personal View/Golwg Bersonol
  ISBN 978-0-86381-470-9

Jean Napier with Alun John Richards
A Tale of Two Rivers   ISBN 978-0-86381-989-1
Two Snowdonia Rivers ISBN 978-0-84527-206-7
The River Conwy   ISBN 978-1-84527-288-3

All published by Gwasg Carreg Gwalch, Llanrwst

This book is dedicated to all who have an appreciation of the history and beauty of Wales

Contents

About Jean Napier

Originally from the East End of London, I have lived in the Snowdonia National Park since 1991 and the magnificent variety of scenery within Eryri and the Llŷn Peninsular is the main inspiration for my work. I am fascinated by man's archaeological and industrial influences on the land and they are a recurring theme in my exhibitions, films and books.

Promoting photography as an artform is my primary motivation; using the camera as a creative tool to explore and interpret, not just a means for recording moments in time.

My work has been widely exhibited in the UK and also in the USA and Australia. I run photography workshops for people of all ages and abilities throughout Wales.

I hold a Masters with Distinction in Fine Art (Photographic & Film Studies) from the University of Wales Aberystwyth.

Jes and me
Photograph by Gill Ray

www.jean-napier.com

Introduction

"A pilgrimage is a journey with meaning. The meaning is in the journeying and in the arrival, in the walking and in the kneeling in prayer at your destination. People make this journey to find rest, refreshment, fulfilment, healing, courage, wholeness and peace."

Clare Williams

This definition of the reasons to go on a pilgrimage by Clare Williams in the foreword of *On Track* by Suzanne Iuppa says it all for me. As I travel through this ancient land I am filled with a sense of harmony and belonging; the act of walking a form of meditation.

I decided to start this journey where I live and finish it at a special place I call my spiritual home. Journeying from St Cadfan's Church in Tywyn to Bardsey Island at the end of the Llŷn Peninsular has been a personal pilgrimage for me. I have enjoyed exploring this part of Wales over a great number of years and found the land endlessly fascinating. Still being able to follow the ancient ways once travelled by man and beast to market, to places of work and worship is so moving!

Along my chosen route, there are many historical features that date back through the centuries. This land abounds with the remains of human habitation: ancient tombs, hillforts, settlements and stone circles, old churches and chapels, to name but a few. Old workings and waste tips from hundreds of derelict mines and quarries – gold, granite, copper, manganese and slate – litter the land, and reveal the extensive industrial activity that once took place here.

This route mainly follows the Coastal Path for ease of access and there are readily available books and maps that are full of information (there is even a phone app of the Path!)

In this small book I have endeavoured to convey to you my passion for this unique land, and give you just a small taste of the wonders that can be discovered here.

This comment by film director, Werner Herzog, on the magic of walking speaks for me – *"The world reveals itself to those that travel on foot"* – welcome to *my* special world.

Jean Napier MA

Historical Time Periods

Neolithic / New Stone Age	4000 – 2400 BC
Bronze Age	2400 – 700 BC
Iron Ages	700 BC – AD 48
Roman Era	43 – 450 AD
Medieval Era (approximate)	500 – 1400 AD

Historical Disclaimer:

During the research for this book I have come across conflicting historical opinions and information pertaining to this part of Wales. When deciding what to include, I have taken into account conversations with local historians and farmers, coupled with my own experience and knowledge of the area.

Photographic Acknowledgements:

The publishers wish to acknowledge their gratitude for these images:
Bywyd Gwyllt Glaslyn Wildlife p 67
Porthmadog Marine Museum p 96
Steve Porter p 111

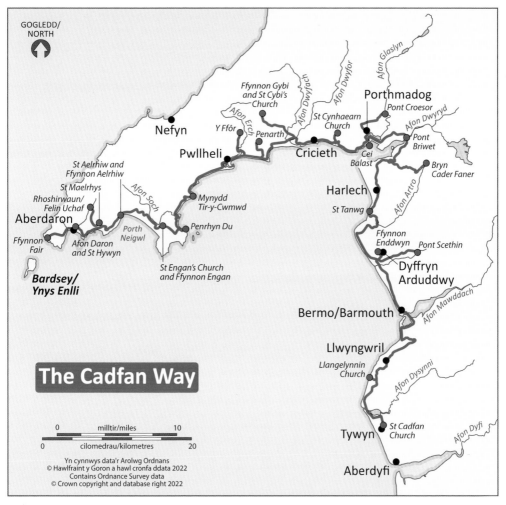

GOGLEDD/
NORTH

*Ffynnon Gybi
and St Cybi's
Church*

Afon Dwyfach

Afon Dwyfor

Afon Glaslyn

Porthmadog

Pont Croesor

Nefyn

Afon Erch

Y Ffôr

Penarth

*St Cynhaearn
Church*

Afon Dwyryd

Pwllheli

Cricieth

*Pont
Briwet*

*Cei
Balast*

*St Aelrhiw and
Ffynnon Aelrhiw*

St Maelrhys

Afon Soch

*Rhoshirwaun/
Felin Uchaf*

*Mynydd
Tir-y-Cwmwd*

*Bryn
Cader Faner*

Harlech

Afon Artro

Aberdaron

*Porth
Neigwl*

Penrhyn Du

St Tanwg

*Ffynnon
Fair*

*Afon Daron
and St Hywyn*

*St Engan's Church
and Ffynnon Engan*

*Ffynnon
Enddwyn*

Pont Scethin

**Dyffryn
Arduddwy**

***Bardsey/
Ynys Enlli***

Afon Mawddach

Bermo/Barmouth

Llwyngwril

*Llangelynnin
Church*

Afon Dysynni

The Cadfan Way

0	milltir/miles	10
0	cilomedrau/kilometres	20

*St Cadfan
Church*

Afon Dyfi

Tywyn

Aberdyfi

Glossary of Welsh Words

Aber	Mouth (of a river)	Hen	Old
Afon	River	Llan	Church, enclosed land
Arfordir	Coast	Llwybr	Path
Bach	Small	Llyn	Lake
Bae	Bay	Maen	Stone
Bryn	Hill	Mawr/Fawr	Great, big
Bwlch	Gap	Melyn	Yellow
Cae	Field	Moel	Round hill
Canolfan	Centre	Morfa	Salt marsh
Carreg	Stone	Mynydd	Mountain
Cefn	Back/Ridge	Ogof	Cave
Ceunant	Gorge	Pen	Top, Head
Clas	Religious settlement	Pentre	Village
Coch	Red	Pont	Bridge
Coed	Trees	Porth	Bay, Port
Croes/Groes	Cross	Pwll	Pool
Du/Ddu	Black	Pistyll	Waterfall
Eglwys	Church	Sarn	Causeway
Chwarel	Quarry	Tan	Below, bottom
Cymru	Wales	Traeth	Beach
Ffordd	Road, Track	Trwyn	Nose (of Rock)/ headland
Ffynnon	Well		
Glas	Blue/Grey	Tŷ	House
Grisiau	Stairs	Tyddyn	Smallholding
Gwyn	White	Ynys	Island

St Cadfan's Church

When I feel the need for some quiet time for contemplation and meditation I often sit in St Cadfan, my local church, with Jes my doggy companion. Around 1,500 years ago, after being banished from Brittany, Cadfan travelled to South Wales with his companions and eventually arrived in Tywyn seeking a place of peace and solitude and here he founded a Christian community to worship God.

The first documentary reference to St Cadfan's Church was in 963, when it is thought to have been the mother church of the region. A 12th century poet, Llywelyn Fardd, described it as a whitewashed building with a ditch surrounding it, beyond which was a clas or lay community, dependent on the church.

By the 13th century St Cadfan's Church became well known as a place of sanctuary and famous for the many miracles that were wrought there.

The site of Ffynnon Gadfan (St Cadfan's well), is situated some 150m

above: Maen Cadfan
right: St Cadfan's Church

to the west-north-west of the church. In 1535 it was located in the churchyard and then enclosed in the 1850s with two baths and four dressing rooms. It became a coach-house and stable in 1890 but a garage is now built over it! The well reputedly cured rheumatism, scrofula and many skin disorders.

Two ancient stones are kept in the church. The first, Maen Cadfan, is believed by scholars to bear the earliest known inscriptions written in the Welsh language and is probably early 9th century. It is inscribed on all four faces with memorials to people who had died and is an artefact of immense national importance. Difficulty in reading the stone caused by weather wear and other damage has made reading and interpretation challenging. After being in several different locations, it was eventually placed in the church around 1844.

The second stone, originally a sundial or mass clock, dates to the 8th or 9th century and was used to mark the times of church services. The top part is missing and would once have

had a rounded top carved with a semi-circular sundial with a later 17th century inscription below and further down can be read *'From Towyn 1 mile'* in 18th century script. The stone was found in rubble after the demolition of Ynysmaengwyn Hall in 1968 and was thought to have served as a gatepost for a pigsty.

Two 14th century effigies are situated in the north wall of the chancel. One of these is of an unnamed priest and the other, a knight, thought to be Gruffydd ab Adda of Dolgoch, who died in 1331. The name 'The Crying Knight' comes from the fact that when the weather is wet, the effigy appears to weep.

Meryl Gover has written an excellent, in depth, book entitled *Cadfan's Church* that contains a comprehensive history of the church and its people through the ages; ideal reading if you are interested to learn more about the church and local history.

left: St Cadfan,
below: Un-named priest & 'Crying Knight'

My Journey

Tywyn to Barmouth

Just next door to the church is the magnificent Magic Lantern Cinema. It has been here since 1893 and was first built as the town's Assembly Rooms. There is proof of film shows here since 1900 with adverts of footage from the Boar War and it was showing films nine years earlier than any other operating cinema in Britain! The cinema is a fantastic asset to **Tywyn** and their repertoire includes live streaming from the RSC and National Theatre plus live comedy and music. For a number of years now they have arranged a meal and entertainment for local people on Christmas Day. I have enjoyed many a themed evening here and we, in Tywyn, are very lucky to have it!

In October 2016 Years 5 and 6 at Ysgol Penybryn, Tywyn Junior School, worked with artist Meri Wells to

left: Magic Lantern Cinema;
above: Ceramic Mural by Ysgol Penybryn;
right: Gwalia Road

produce a beautiful ceramic mural commemorating the 1500 year anniversary of St Cadfan establishing his Christian community in Tywyn. The pupils also put together an illustrated book of their drawings and made a full-size replica of the Cadfan Stone. Every two years the school undertakes an art project that incorporates the life and work of St Cadfan.

My journey begins travelling north along Gwalia Road towards the Broadwater, a salt-water lagoon that was formed by the Dysynni estuary when it became silted up in the 19th century. It is a haven for many wetland birds and is designated a Site of Special Scientific Interest (SSSI). Fabulous views up the valley to Cader Idris can be seen all along the Broadwater. The new bridge over the Dysynni was lifted into place in January 2013 thus making it possible to follow the coast instead of having to take an 8-mile detour inland. The previous Bailey Bridge that linked the two military camps was dismantled after their closure in the 1960s.

The Coastal Path skirts **Tonfanau** granite quarry that opened in 1892. Its claim to fame was that it was thought to be the hardest granite in Europe. On the lower levels are the remains of limekilns dating back to the early days of the quarry and the lower slurry looks like the outflow from a volcano. A steam railway brought the granite from the quarry to the Cambrian Coast Railway in 1898 and the quarry was taken over by John Corbett of Ynysmaengwyn in 1906 until 1965. The seafront houses in Marine Parade in Tywyn were built using granite from the quarry as were the granite curbstones laid on the High Street. It ceased work in 1998 but still produces local rock on a very small scale mainly for repairing roads.

The remains of the once huge Tonfanau army camp are visible below. Established in 1937, in anticipation of the Second World War, anti-aircraft gunners trained here firing at targets towed by planes from Morfa Airfield. At one time there were 260 accommodation blocks mostly of brick, a hospital, three 600-seater dining rooms and a 1000-seater theatre! In 1940 with the threat of invasion the camp was switched from training to frontline defense. Boys

above: Tonfanau Army Camp;
top right: Trig Point; below: Broadwater

aged 15 to 17 belonging to the All Arms Junior Leaders Regiment started training here in 1959 to become non-commissioned officers. It was reopened in 1972, six years after closing, to host 1,500 refugees from Uganda after Idi Amin expelled the Asian population.

High Above Tonfanau is Tal y Garreg hill fort, a large earthwork

enclosure. The date is uncertain but thought to be Iron Age. It covers an oval area with two sets of ditches and ramparts and would have been a good place to watch out for any enemy approaching for miles around. Over time, the quarry below has eaten into the west side of the fort creating sheer cliffs on one side and care needs to be taken on the steep paths. It is worth the climb as the views inland and across Cardigan Bay from the top are breathtaking, with Bardsey Island

visible to the northwest, and even St David's to the southwest on a clear day. The highest point at 178 metres is called Beacon Hill where a Trig Point made of local stone is situated. The Beacon, an important navigation aid for shipping, used to exist at this point; once maintained by Trinity House, only the remains of the wooden supports can be seen now.

Rhoslefain beach, further round the coast, was once used by smugglers to bring in salt and the aptly named Carreg yr Halen (halen: *salt*) is where they landed. Irish salt producers were paid £1 per ton but an extortionate £12 tax per ton was added on to raise revenue for the Crown. Thankfully the tax was finally abolished in 1825. Nearby is Glyndŵr's Cave where it is said Owain Glyndŵr hid from his English pursuers after his defeat by Henry IV. It is marked on the OS Map as Ogof Owain.

Following along ancient pathways through Rhoslefain, the Coastal Path now climbs high above the main road.

An offshoot branches down to **Llangelynnin Old Church** dedicated to St Celynnin who lived in the 6th century. The current church dates from the 13th century with 17th century wall paintings that show post-medieval pieces of text and on the west wall is a 'memento mori', the figure of Death rediscovered in 2003. It shows a skeletal figure holding a

below: Owain Glyndŵr's Cave;
right: Salt Rock

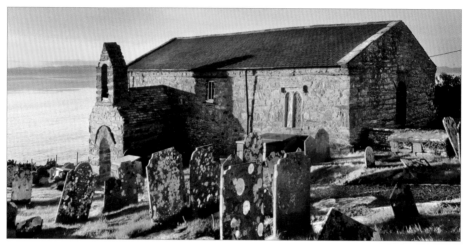

scythe standing over a grave in which a skull and bones can be seen; probably painted in the 16th or 17th century. The benches are inscribed with the occupants' names and arranged by order of class and influence – sixteen of the pews still bear a personal name followed by that of the farm. Those named "*Clerk's Seat*" and "*Pigyallt Charity*" indicate reserved seats. A very rare survival is the wooden double horse-brier that was used for the ease of transportation of the dead from remote farms to the churchyard for burial.

The parish register records over 2500 burials from 1618, a large number for such a small patch of ground; most are unmarked and only a few took place after 1842. The 19th century register recorded burials from wrecks off the coast and also unidentified bodies washed up on the beach. A gravestone nearest to the sea is inscribed:

Sacred
To the Memory of
William Thomas Aged 15
Who unfortunately drowned in the shipwreck
Of the Brig 'Elizabeth' in Cardigan Bay
On a voyage from Liverpool to Jamaica

Abram Wood, the gypsy king was buried here in November 1799. His numerous descendents included several celebrated Welsh harpists of the 19th century.

The Coastal Path runs eastwards high above Bae Ceredigion (*Cardigan Bay*) along an ancient track that passes the remains of Pant Gwyn – a drovers' inn –and Castell y Gaer – an Iron Age fort. It then drops down to **Llwyngwril**. Llwyngwril had close links with the Quakers who came here in great numbers to avoid religious persecution in the 17th century. Owen Humphreys of Llwyn Du gifted the land for Bryn Tallwyn, the Quaker burial ground that overlooks the

above: Pant Gwyn; below: Priest hole;
right: Quaker's Burial Ground;
far right: Old milestone

beach, probably in 1664. There is a priest hole hidden in the loft of Llwyn Du and Quaker meetings were held in the main room. It is believed that two escape tunnels exist that ran from the house, one leading to Hendre Hall and another to the beach. Nearly half the Quakers that left Wales for Pennsylvania in the 17th century came from Meirionnydd. Harrington House,

a house in Pennsylvania, was built on land bequeathed by William Penn (the founder of the American refuge) to the same Cruickshank design as Llwyn Du.

Ffordd Sarnau leads up from Llwyngwril, an offshoot from Ffordd Du, one of an ancient network of mountain routes thought to be part of a Roman Road network. A large number of cairns, prehistoric stones, hut circles and settlements can be found alongside the road and, on a lower slope, are the distinctive remains of a Romano British hut circle settlement.

It is then a steep descent down to the massive Golwern and Henddol Slate Quarries with fantastic views of the Mawddach and Barmouth far below. Dr George Walker, a Nottingham surgeon renowned as a sanitary reformer, opened Golwern in 1867 and he provided employment for many local people over a period of twenty-five years. Slate was brought

left: Golwern Slate Quarry; right: Arthog Bog

down a long incline and then taken by cart to Barmouth Ferry Station on Afon Mawddach. The quarries finally closed in about 1920.

The Blue Lake, a 40-foot quarry pit deliberately filled with water in 1901 by an engineer employed by Arthur McDougal (the flour millionaire) in a scheme to provide **Fairbourne** with electricity can still be viewed from above with care. Once a popular swimming spot, the current landowner recently closed off the tunnel entrance as too many visitors were leaving loads of rubbish here. The lake gets its distinctive blue colour from the copper impurities in the slate. Unfortunately the scheme to provide electricity was not realized.

The main line railway, a major feat of engineering, runs halfway along the steep cliffs just before Friog. An accident happened here in 1883 and a similar one in 1930 when the engine crashed onto the beach below.

Fairbourne owes its existence to Arthur McDougal who was looking for

a country estate in the area and conceived of building a seaside resort to be called South Barmouth. Fairbourne takes its name from the new railway station McDougal built in 1899. In July 1895 he purchased a substantial acreage including the Ynysfaig estate by the Mawddach but his ambitious plans were thwarted by overwhelming competition from the better facilities in Barmouth and he sold the estate in 1912.

Along the beachhead are a few remaining WW2 tank traps placed here in 1940. Originally several hundred, they were known as dragon's teeth and are one of the finest surviving anti-invasion lines in the UK, nearly all in their original positions. I used to tell young people from Outward Bound that these were old trig points that had been retired from the top of mountains!

Fairbourne Tramway, now the Fairbourne Miniature Railway, was

left: WW2 tank traps; right: Barmouth Bridge

originally a two-mile long horse-drawn construction initially built in 1895 to carry building materials and extended to the ferry at Porth Penrhyn in 1898. It was paid for by McDougal and was converted to a 15-inch gauge steam railway in 1916 and again in 1986 to its present gauge of two foot.

Further along the coast is Y Fawnog (also called Arthog Bog) a small RSPB wetland nature reserve situated southeast of Morfa Mawddach Station just off the Mawddach Trail. It is a remnant of a vast bog that once covered much of the Mawddach estuary and is a rare and precious habitat home to numerous special plants and wildlife species. In springtime there is a wonderful display of wildflowers and over 130 species have been recorded. Cuckoos and a whole range of warblers can also be seen and heard. In the 19th century, peat was cut from here for fuel and taken away by sailing ship. The ground can be rough and very wet in winter and the RSPB are overcoming the problem of rank growth by allowing ponies to graze on the land at certain times of the year.

At the west end of the Mawddach Trail is **Barmouth** Bridge, the major crossing over the Mawddach. It is the longest timber viaduct in Wales and stretches for half a mile and one of the oldest in regular use in Britain. Work began in 1864 and it was opened in 1867. As the bridge neared completion, passengers were taken over by horse-and-carriage. It consists of 113 spans and is supported by over 300 timber piles. The original drawbridge to allow for the traffic of ships was replaced in 1899 by the current steel swing bridge that required eight men to operate manually. Over the years it has needed extensive repairs, the latest completed in 2021. It is part of the National Cycle Route 8 as well as being a favourite walkway across to Barmouth from Morfa Mawddach Station.

A ferry was established in 1569, barely a year into the reign of Elizabeth I, and initially run by local monks. In the 1860s there were two ferries; one for passengers and one for animals and wheeled vehicles. A passenger ferry between Barmouth and Port Penrhyn still runs in the summer.

The view up the Mawddach is spectacular and poet John Ruskin is claimed to have said that only one other journey in the world had views to compare with the one from Dolgellau to Barmouth, and that was the journey from Barmouth to Dolgellau.

left: Fairbourne ferry; right: Afon Mawddach

Barmouth to Harlech

Between 1750 and 1865 a total of 318 ships were built along the Mawddach as oak growing along the riverbanks was especially suitable for shipbuilding. Barmouth became a major port and the harbour was dredged in 1797 to make it safer and more accessible for shipping. The wool trade was an important trade in Meirionnydd and in 1772 a depot was established here. Long pieces of white cloth, known as webs, were sold as clothing for slaves and regularly exported to North America. The coming of the railway in 1860 saw the gradual demise of the shipping trade.

The Seamen's Mission, a zinc hut by the old harbour, was built in 1890 to offer shelter and comfort to sailors. It was restored in 1984 and is the only one to have survived in Wales. Open to the public, it is an interesting building to visit containing an exhibition of old photographs, models of ships, listings of rescues by the Lifeboat and newspaper cuttings.

Frank Cocksey's beautifully carved fishermen's sculpture placed at the pierhead, was cut from Cararra marble that originally came from Italy and was salvaged from an early 18th century shipwreck discovered five miles north of Barmouth.

The highlight of the maritime year in June is the start of the Three Peaks Race which first ran in 1977. It demands that teams of five (three seamen and two runners) sail up the west coast of Britain, pausing successively to land at Caernarfon (to climb Snowdon), Whitehaven (to climb Scarfell) and Fort William (to climb Ben Nevis), covering 389 miles by boat, 18 miles of cycling, 72 miles of running and a total of 14,000 feet gain in height! Phew!

By 1834, increasing crime in Barmouth called for the erection of a 'Round House' containing two cells; one for men and one for women. Named Tŷ Crwn, it was to house

'*drunkards, slatterns and ne'er-do-wells*' who were disturbing the peace. Tradition says it was built round so that the devil had no corner to hide in! In such lockups, a common feature of Welsh towns, the Parish Constable could, without recourse to judges or magistrates, summarily incarcerate any citizen manifesting signs of obstreperousness.

Dinas Oleu, situated just above the town, was the first piece of land (4.5 acres) to be given to the National Trust donated by Mrs Fanny Talbot in 1895 and a stone platform was built in 1995 to commemorate the 100th anniversary. In 1874 she also donated twelve cottages and another 4.5 acres to the art critic John Ruskin for his project the Guild of St George. Set up to promote art, craft and the rural environment, it is now a registered educational charity. A major celebration was held in 2019 to mark 200 years since Ruskin's birth. One of Ruskin's first tenants was Auguste Guyard, a frenchman, who taught local people the virtues of a frugal, industrious life until his death in 1883; he is buried up on the hillside.

Another artist appreciator of the local landscape, poet William Wordsworth, described Barmouth in 1824 "*With a fine sea view in front, the mountains behind, the glorious estuary running eight miles inland and Cader Idris within compass of a day's walk of Barmouth, can always hold its own against any rival*".

Leaving Barmouth, a short distance inland from **Llanaber**, is the upland area of Mynydd Egryn that features a number of ancient sites and monuments of significant archaeological interest. The National Trust have produced a leaflet which outlines a circular walk of about four miles starting from Egryn Abbey taking in the prehistoric Pen Dinas hill fort and a whole string of standing stones, hut circles and tombs. Carneddau Hengwm is the most spectacular and

above: Carneddau Hengwm;
below: Stone Circle

The Cadfan Way – A Journey from Tywyn to Bardsey

consists of three Neolithic burial chambers dated about 3000 BC, one of which has survived more or less intact. A Bronze Age ring cairn is situated further along the track with distinctive outward leaning stones – possibly used for burial and ceremonial purposes.

Further north, inland from **Tal-y-bont**, is the remote Yscethin valley, also strewn with the evidence of early civilization. A walk through the valley passes Corsygedol Hall, an old manor house and Cromlech Corsygedol yet another Neolithic burial chamber. Due to the huge amount of stones nearby, the tomb is thought to have originally been at least 84 feet long and 44 feet wide.

Towering over the valley is Craig y Dinas, an impressive Iron Age Hill Fort with the remains of a round house settlement inside and Bardsey Island can be seen in the distance from the apex of the fort, a good vantage point

top left: Craig y Dinas; bottom left: Pont Yscethin; below: Cromlech Corsygedol

above: Neolithic burial chambers; below: Scots Pines; right: Morfa Dyffryn

for watching out for approaching enemies. Due to its massive size, it is thought that the fort was also a place of refuge or a communal meeting place. The track eventually leads to Pont Scethin, a magnificent 16th century bridge.

The nearby Scots pines marked the route for the drovers, and the path from Tal-y-bont is an old drovers way. My book entitles *Rhinogydd Ancient*

Routes and Old Roads contains a comprehensive history of the drovers and the local area.

At **Dyffryn Ardudwy** just behind the school are two more Neolithic burial chambers dating from early 3000 BC that are among the earliest tombs built in Britain; one contained evidence of a late Bronze Age cremation and another both Neolithic and Bronze Age pottery and a stone pendant. Such tombs were originally covered with stones or earth but left exposed after being plundered by grave robbers. The enormous concentration of Bronze Age monuments and settlements in this area indicate its importance in prehistoric times.

The Coastal Path runs along the beach through Morfa Dyffryn, a National Nature Reserve with access to the 2½-mile beach via a board-walk. Because of its bare sand dunes, it is one of the most important dune systems in Wales. They are becoming increasingly rare and provide habitat for highly specialized plants that include wild orchids and marsh hellebore, and

animals such as the brown hare and a variety of reptiles. If you are so inclined, part of the beach is designated for naked sunbathing and swimming – there are large warning signs!

Inland from Dyffryn is the beautiful Ffynnon Enddwyn holy well; tradition says that Saint Enddwyn bathed and refreshed herself here and was cured from a '*sore disease*'. It is said to cure arthritis, rheumatism and skin diseases and it was a tradition to drink the water

left: Morfa Dyffryn; right: Ffynnon Enddwyn

and apply some of the moss as a plaster. People have been known to leave their crutches and sticks behind to show their restoration to health. I have often drunk the water and, to date, have no arthritis or skin diseases!

On the coast at **Llandanwg** is a Grade 2 listed church dedicated to **St Tanwg** who was a member of St Cadfan's retinue. The church is partially buried in the dunes and only

20m from the high water mark. In a terrible storm in the 19th century the sea smashed the wall of the cemetery and the gravestones were buried under great mounds of sand. The earliest parts of the church are thought to date back to the 13th century making it one of the oldest Christian sites in Britain and the longest continuing place of Christian worship with services still being held today. The grave of Welsh

above left: St Tanwg; below: Tremadog Bay; right: Afon Artro

poet Siôn Phylip lies in the churchyard; he lived nearby on Shell Island but drowned crossing the Dwyryd to Llandanwg in 1620. In the 1840s the church was abandoned and soon fell into disrepair; the church filled with sand and fishermen hung their nets on the altar rail. Since then restoration work has been carried out on various occasions with the last in 1987 costing £20,000.

Inland from Llandanwg is Chwarel Hen/Old Llanfair Slate Quarry situated above the meadows of Cae Cethin, an ancient farm. First opening in 1873 when the slate industry was at its peak, the quarry produced slate for 33 years until its closure in 1906. When in full production forty men were employed here; the quarrymen and rockmen worked by candlelight, their candle simply a length of cotton dipped repeatedly into mutton fat.

The caverns hewn out by the quarrymen are now open to the public and a souvenir guide shows a detailed plan of the nine chambers with full information about each one. Given a safety helmet and torch I was free to explore two levels of these amazing galleries (softly lit) that are just as the quarrymen left them. With a café, shop and farm for children it is a grand day out and my visit an informative and enjoyable experience.

I was shown into a secret slate chamber where 20 tons of Dragon Cheese is slowly maturing. It includes their specialty handcrafted Slate Cavern-aged Cheddar infused with Penderyn whisky aged in Madeira casks – yummy!

Harlech to Cricieth

Harlech Castle, one of the most spectacular in Britain, sits high up on a 200-foot vertical rocky crag overlooking the dunes below. It is thought that a fortress of a military character was first built here by Maelgwyn Gwynedd sometime in the 6th century and Collwyn ap Tango, Lord of Llŷn and Ardudwy, resided in a square tower of the original building in the 11th century, the remains of which can still be seen.

The current castle was erected immediately after the conquest of Wales by Edward 1st. Completed in just 7 years between 1283 and 1290, the work cost more that £8,000. Money, in gold, to pay for the construction was kept at Cymer Abbey near Dolgellau. The castle was protected by the sea from the west and a huge moat on the landward side. During a seven-year siege in 1294 by Madog ap Llywelyn, the defenders were able to hold out as they were supplied by ship from Ireland via the 108 stone steps leading down to the sea. Harlech was besieged in 1404 and eventually fell into the hands of Owain Glyndŵr who used it as a base until 1409. After a fierce bombardment under the command of the future King Henry V that destroyed the southern and eastern parts of the outer walls, the castle surrendered in 1409.

'Two king's' sculpture

Just outside the castle is a sculpture named *The Two Kings* by Ivert Robert-Jones (1913-1996). Unveiled in 1984, it depicts the Mabinogion story of Branwen, a Welsh Princess, and is a lament on the folly and carnage of war. It shows Bendigeidfran, King of Britain and Branwen's brother, carrying the body of his nephew Boy King Gwern following his death at the hands of Efnisien; it symbolizes the sorrowful burden that love can bring; Harlech was the seat of King Bendigeidfran.

W. M. Condry's comment about the castle is spot on: "*It is one of the great view points of Wales. The foreground is a curving sandy shore four miles long with waves ever moving in towards the dunes of Morfa Harlech colourful and fragrant with wildflowers, mosses, lichens and fungi.*"

Harlech, until very recently, was named as having the steepest street in the world verified by the Guinness Book of Records. Ffordd Pen Lech, with a gradient of 37.45%, is hard work and I have walked up it many times albeit very slowly!

Leading north along the beach around **Harlech** is the impressive Morfa Harlech, a National Nature Reserve which is one of the most important actively growing dune systems in Britain. In spring and summer you can see the three-coloured dune pansy, the pyramidal orchid and even the scarce bee orchid. When in flower, the dune grasslands are home to a number of butterflies and moths such as the six-spot burnet moth, common blue and small copper butterflies. It is the home for rare insects such as mining bees and solitary wasps that depend on the bare sand, and sand lizards abound. Ringed plovers nest on the beach so care needs to be taken not to disturb them or the skylarks and stonechat breeding in the dunes.

Together with Morfa Dyffryn they form an almost continuous area of sand dunes all along the coastline.

The Coastal Path then heads to **Ynys** situated on the Afon Dwyryd. A fantastic panorama of the mountains of Snowdonia, including Snowdon/Yr Wyddfa, can be seen looking north over the marsh with Portmeirion visible across the river and Borth-y-Gest in the distance.

At the beginning of Glastraeth salt marsh is Tŷ Gwyn Mawr, an early 19th century warehouse once used to store corn ferried across Traeth Bach. It was also a stopping off point for ferry passengers, an informal public house and gathering place for locals. A rare

Tŷ Gwyn Mawr

example of a coastal building that combines warehouse and dwelling, it is now a private house. In August 1862 a ferry carrying nine passengers returning from Porthmadog to Ynys sank half way across as the wind picked up making it impossible for the pilot to control the boat causing the ferry to fill with water. Only the ferry owner and one of the passengers could be saved by another ferry.

High above **Talsarnau,** on the north-west side of the Rhinogydd mountain ridge, is Bryn Cader Faner ('the crown of thorns') the most spectacular Bronze Age stone circle I have ever visited for both its magnificence and location and well worth the uphill journey to visit it. Situated at the junction of two ancient tracks, it can be seen from afar and is thought to be the burial site of an important person containing a *cist* (grave) in the centre. Before the Second World War the British Army removed some of the stones and those remaining were used as target practice! Luckily it survived this modern-day sacrilege more or less intact but only 18 of the tall outer circle stones are left instead of the original count thought to be nearer 30.

Situated on the Dwyryd near **Llandecwyn** station are the remains of quays where small boats collected slate brought upriver from Blaenau

below: Bryn Cader Faner;
top right: Slate Quay; below: Ynys Cyngar

Ffestiniog by horse drawn carts. The slate was then shipped out to larger vessels anchored at Ynys Cyngar by the mouth of the Glaslyn for onward shipping to Liverpool and it is estimated that over 420,000 tons of slates were exported from these quays. Due to the vast expense of all this trans-shipment, the Ffestiniog quarries were at a huge monetary disadvantage compared to other quarries that were served by tramways that lead straight down to the sea.

The original Pont Briwet, a Victorian road and railway viaduct spanning the Dwyryd by Llandecwyn station, was made of pine shipped from the Baltic with twenty-two evenly spaced piers supported on massive timber piles driven into the estuary. As the condition of the bridge deteriorated over time, a replacement structure was built alongside and it was proposed that the original be used for pedestrians. Considered structurally unsafe due to being weakened by the work carried out whilst building the new bridge, it was demolished in 2014. The new bridge initially opened for rail in 2014 and road traffic in July 2015.

Just north of Pont Briwet near Llandecwyn Station is the entrance to Gwaith Powdr, a post-industrial nature reserve. From its opening in 1865 until closure in 1995, this remote location with its steep-sided valleys made it the perfect place for the manufacture of explosives that were in great demand for the slate and coal mining industry.

During the Second World War over 17 million grenades were produced here. Production of specific types of explosives, such as nitroglycerine, peaked in the 1970s and at this time the site was considered to be the most sophisticated operation of its kind in the world. Work finally ceased in 1976 following a decline in the need for these explosives. The site was then

left: Pont Briwet;
above: Gwaith Powdr Nature Reserve

decontaminated and decommissioned prior to its handover to the North Wales Wildlife Trust.

Since the Wildlife Trust took over the site, it has become a haven for wildlife due to the wide-ranging habitats found here which include open heath land, grassy glades and the steep-sided wooded valley. The remains of brick and stone buildings and tunnels are the ideal places for the lesser horseshoe bats to roost. What is now a bird hide at one time housed seven settling tanks where excess nitroglycerine was removed from the washing water. The woodland is the place to see pied flycatchers and tree pipits and the glades abound with wild flowers in the summer.

Following around the coast is **Penrhyndeudraeth**, named around the mid 19th century from its location on a promontory between two shores, Traeth Mawr and Traeth Bach. The upper part of the village, previously

left & right: Ffestiniog Union Workhouse

called 'Cefn Coch', was situated above a vast swamp with large stagnant pools.

Like many small villages in the area, ways to earn a living at that time included work in agriculture, as servants in smallholdings, knitting stockings and fishing, therefore the opening of the gunpowder works employing hundreds of men and women created a much needed boom in employment.

The now dilapidated Ffestiniog Union Workhouse in Penrhyndeudraeth was built in 1839. The Poor Law Commissioners authorized an expenditure of £3,200 for its construction to accommodate 150 inmates. In 1875 more buildings were added including infectious, vagrant and receiving wards and an able-bodied men's dormitory. The vagrants' accommodation had six combined sleeping/working cells where inmates slept on wire metal beds without a mattress. The work cells had a metal grid on the outside through which

stones broken down by the inmates were passed through. In 1918 part of the premises was used for the accommodation of adult 'mental deficients'. 1948 saw it join the NHS as Bron-y-Garth Hospital and I remember going there for foot treatment in the mid 1990s. It finally closed its doors in 2009 and is now privately owned.

Portmeirion, designed and built between 1925 and 1927 by Sir Clough Williams-Ellis in the style of an Italian village, is situated on the estuary of the Dwyryd; the site was originally an 18th century foundry and boatyard. Run as a hotel, it is a constant source of inspiration for writers and television producers. Noel Coward wrote Blithe Spirit while staying here and the site has been used as a location for numerous films and television shows. I rushed home on a Friday evening in the late 1960s to catch episodes of the famous "*The Prisoner*" staring Patrick McGoohan – it was a shame that the final episode was so disappointing and left many questions unanswered as to what was going on!

The coming of the Ffestiniog Railway eventually connected many of the slate quarries to **Porthmadog** via inclines and tramways thus alleviating much of the transportation expense and tonnage in 1863 increased to 64,093.

Crossing the Glaslyn towards Porthmadog, the Cob, a man-made causeway, was completed in 1811 after four years of construction and the embankment was part of a grand plan by William Alexander Madocks who owned land in Traeth Mawr. His aim was to control the flow of the Glaslyn and drain it permanently for the land to be used for agriculture. Madocks died almost bankrupt on his European travels and is buried in Paris. He did not live long enough to see the advantage of the Cob for the slate industry as, in 1832, an Act of Parliament authorized construction of

left: Portmeirion; below: The Cob

a railway from Blaenau Ffestiniog to Porthmadog that crossed the Cob. This diversion of the Glaslyn caused it to scour out a new natural harbour deep enough to allow passage for small ocean-going sailing ships. In 1825 the first public wharves appeared and by 1873 over 116,000 tones of slate were exported. This led to a vast expansion in Porthmadog and its population grew from 885 in 1821 to over 3,000 by 1861.

left: Boston Lodge; right: Llyn Bach

Situated at the southeast end of the Cob is Boston Lodge Halt, named after Boston in Lincolnshire where Maddocks was an MP. It is the engineering works of the Ffestiniog and Welsh Highland Railway and has been in operation for over 150 years. A vast amount of restoration and repair work is carried out here on both locomotives and carriages. Their expertise in the field of railway engineering is renowned and London Underground Museum chose Boston Lodge to restore Metropolitan Railway Carriage 353 from its use as a garden shed into as-new condition for its 150th anniversary in 2013.

Llyn Bach, a tidal lagoon, was formed when the embankments to contain the Glaslyn were built. It has become a haven for wildlife and migrating birds with oystercatchers, redshanks and curlews commonly seen here. The view of the Moelwynion mountain range across the lagoon is superb on a clear day.

The Maritime Museum, situated on the harbour, occupies the last remaining slate warehouse built in the mid 19th century. It is a fascinating place displaying tools, illustrations, ship models and objects from wrecked ships, and also shows a comprehensive video of the history of shipping and its links to the slate industry in Porthmadog.

Close by the Cob is **Cei Balast**, an artificial island formed from ballast dumped by incoming ships. This

consisted of rocks, sand, bricks and gravel from all around the world. A quay where unloading could take place here was built in 1862 by three brothers, Joseph, John and Evan Lewis, and the wooden skeletons of the jettys are still there. I have been over to the island on numerous occasions by fording the Glaslyn from below the railway embankment but care must be taken to only cross at low tide and when the river flow is low.

The Dwyryd and Glaslyn meet at **Borth-y-Gest** and ships were constructed here long before Porthmadog was established. 'Pilot houses' were built here to accommodate pilots whose local knowledge was imperative to guide ships around the treacherous ever-changing sand banks.

Just inland from Porthmadog, at Pont Croesor on the Glaslyn, is the Glaslyn Osprey Visitors Centre, a small charity run by a group of wildlife

left: Cei Balast; top right: Borth-y-Gest; below: Osprey

enthusiasts. The centre is opened when the ospreys arrive back from Africa, usually around the beginning of April. Fixed cameras focus on a nest further upriver sending film footage back to screens at the centre where all the action from the birds first arriving, egg-sitting, through to the chicks fledging, can be seen and is well worth a visit!

Morfa Bychan is the home of the famous Black Rock Sands (Traeth Morfa Bychan) that stretch for over

sited in a remote walled churchyard raised above the marsh at the end of an ancient causeway. St Cynhaearn was a man of high birth who embarked on a monastic life following the death of his father at the hands of the Saxons. It is said that he rowed out to an island on Llyn Ystumllyn in the 7th century and there decided to build his church. The oldest parts of the church are the 12th

left: Thrift;
below & right: St Cynhaearn Church

two miles from Ynys Cyngar to Cricieth and one of the few beaches where vehicles are allowed. The name comes from Graig Ddu (Black Rock) the colour of an upland area to the west. At low tide rock pools and large caves can be explored along the northwest end of the beach and the caves contain the most amazing multi-coloured bands of rock strata at ninety-degree angles to each other.

On a footpath northeast of the Coastal Path is **St Cynhaearn Church**

century nave and the north and south transepts were added in the 16th century.

There are two graves of interest in the churchyard, one is David Owen, a famous harpist and composer, known as Dafydd y Garreg Wen (the name of his farm nearby). A beautiful harp is carved in relief on his tombstone.

The other grave is that of Jack Black (Du), or John Ystumllyn the name on his gravestone. He was captured in Africa circa 1742 and the young black man arrived at Ystumllyn House in the mid 18th century as a gift to the Wynne family. He became a proficient gardener and the love of his life was the maid, Margaret Gruffydd. When she moved away he absconded from Ystumllyn to meet up with her and they married in Dolgellau. He later returned to Ystumllyn for a while and on retirement was given land and property by Ellis Wynne. He died at the age of 46 of jaundice and his death is recorded as 1786 – although his gravestone says 1791.

Cricieth to Aberdaron

Cricieth Castle stands on a headland high above the town in a strategic setting overlooking Tremadog Bay. Originally a stronghold of the Welsh princes, it was built by Llywelyn Fawr (Fawr: *the Great*) between 1230 and 1240. Captured by Edward 1's forces in 1283, it was then extensively fortified including the adaptation of one of the towers for the use of a catapult. The castle withstood a siege led by Madog ap Llywelyn in 1295 mainly because it was being reprovisioned by sea. The Welsh leader Owain Glyndŵr captured and burnt the castle in 1404 and the walls still bear evidence of scorching. It was gifted to the government by Lord Harlech in 1933.

David Lloyd George, a Cricieth solicitor, was elected as Liberal MP for the Caernarfon Boroughs in 1890. He held the seat for 55 years during which time he was Prime Minister from 1916

HWYN AC A DRY ADNO DAU PRYD

Memorial Hall commemorative tiles

to 1922. One of the great welfare reformers of the 20th century, he started pensions and unemployment payments, and his position brought Cricieth new status of international prominence. He was known as '*the man who won the war*', through his brilliant administration and leadership skills. He also negotiated the Peace Treaty of Versailles.

He married Margaret Owen in 1888, even though her father initially disapproved of him, and they had five children. In 1918 she received the Grand Cross of the Order of the British Empire after raising over £200,000 for war charities. She was a Welsh humanitarian and one of the first women magistrates appointed in Britain in 1919. A shelter donated by her stands on the Green at West Parade in Cricieth.

The Memorial Hall was opened by Lloyd George in 1922 and celebrated its

Centenery Year in June 2022. It was built with public donations in memory of local residents who fought and perished during the First World War and a memorial now includes those who gave their lives in the Second World War. Lloyd George laid the foundation stone and is quoted as saying "*I felt it was my duty to come here to pay my tribute of respect to these fine young men for their fine deeds and their fine sacrifice*". The beautiful black-and-white tiles that line the pathway to the door were laid in 2019 in commemoration of the Second World War.

The Lloyd George Museum is situated in the centre of **Llanystumdwy** north of the Coastal Path. It is also possible to visit nearby Highgate, the house where he was brought up as a child. The museum was founded in 1948 three years after his death from cancer, and contains a comprehensive display of objects telling his story. These include medals, paintings, pictures, photographs,

left: Lloyd George's grave; above: St Gybi's Well

personal items, documents and even a draft copy of the Conditions of Peace at Versailles.

A short walk from the museum is Lloyd George's grave. A site chosen by Lloyd George, it was designed by Clough Williams-Ellis, a lifelong friend, and is situated on a bank of the Dwyfor. Inside a stone gateway the grave consists of a large boulder set in an oval enclosure with two slate plaques that record his name and the years of his birth and death.

Further northwest is **Llangybi** where, in a quiet secluded spot behind St Cybi's churchyard, is Ffynnon Gybi (ffynnon: *well*).

A reference to healing wells linked to the early saints was written by Erasmus Saunders, a priest and writer in the 18th century:

"And there being not only Churches and Chapels but Springs and Fountains dedicated to those

Saints, they do at certain times go and bathe themselves in them and do sometimes leave some small oblations behind them"

It is dedicated to Cybi who was a 6th century saint reputed to have lived in the area; but the well's sacred status is probably pre-Christian. The water has long been believed to hold healing properties for a variety of conditions that include warts, lameness, blindness, scurvy and rheumatism to name but a few! Erected in the early 1700s, it is one of the sturdiest structures of its kind in North Wales and consists of two well chambers, a caretaker's cottage and a small-detached latrine building. Inside the main well-chamber there are a series of large niches set into the walls that probably once contained statues of saints and the Virgin Mary. There is a beautiful feeling of peace and serenity here. It is a special place for contemplation as well as a great spot for a picnic!

St Cybi's Church is dedicated to the 6th century Saint Cybi who was believed to have been an early missionary. It is said that he struck a stone nearby thus causing the flow of water that became one of the most famous healing wells of Wales. It is a well-preserved largely medieval Grade 2 listed building with a late 15th century chancel that was restored in 1879.

Further west on the Peninsular is the market town of **Pwllheli**. The name

left: St Cybi's Church; *top right*: Penlan Fawr Inn; *below*: Pwllheli Harbour

means *'salt water pool'* which originated from a low-lying piece of land that was flooded by the sea at high tide. Fishermen and their families were probably the first people to settle here.

Originally ships would anchor on the beach for loading but, as ships grew larger in the 18th century, a new quay needed to be constructed and by the middle of the 19th century Pwllheli had become a major shipbuilding centre.

Penlan Fawr Inn is the oldest building in Pwllheli and thought to

date from the 16th century; records from 1784 show that the building was an inn at that time. One of the arguments put forward in 1892 for non-closure of the inn was that an ancient tradition existed of playing games in one of the rooms. Over the years many activities took place and in 1802 the Rev John Hughes of Brecon, the first Wesleyan to visit Pwllheli, preached here. At that time it was also school as well as an inn.

A single-track horse-drawn tramway was built in 1890, one of many developed by Solomon Andrews (head of a tram-operating company based in Cardiff) that originally ran from Pwllheli Town Centre to the West End promenade on the seafront. Its initial use was to carry stone for the construction of the seawall and the Parade. In 1896 Andrews purchased an estate at **Llanbedrog** that included Glyn y Weddw, a large Victorian house, and the tramway was further extended here via the coast in 1897.

Close to the beach at Llanbedrog,

Plas Glyn y Weddw is an impressive gothic-style mansion built in 1857 initially for the art collection of Elizabeth, widow of Sir Love Jones-Parry; this family was a major landowner on the Llŷn. Now named Oriel Plas Glyn y Weddw Art Centre, it is one of Wales' oldest art venues.

In June 2003 the statue of '*Louise*', a life-size figurative bronze by David Williams Ellis, and a gift from Sir Kyffin Williams, was stolen from its three-ton stone plinth in a night-time raid.

left: Old tram; above: The Iron Man; below: 'Louise'

Luckily it was handed into Pwllheli Police Station just three days later after it appeared on Crimestoppers television programme – presumably being too hot to handle!

The Coastal Path climbs steeply up through woodland to where the Iron Man (or woman!) stands looking out over Cardigan Bay. Created by local craftsmen David and Hugh Jones, it was helicoptered into position in June

2002. The original statue was a wooden figurehead, erected in 1919, that came from a shipwreck just off the headland below.

The Coastal Path skirts around the Mynydd and then drops down to the beach under the cliffs. Along the bottom of the cliff are three enormous disused granite quarries; granite being of great commercial importance in the late 19th century.

Traeth Ty'n Tywyn stretches westwards from the remains of the quarries to **Abersoch** where the Coastal Path runs along the top of the beach at Mean High Water. The Lifeboat Station was initially sited at Penrhyn Du further round the coast, the original boathouse cost £170 in 1869. A year later the station received its first silver medal when it was awarded to Rev Owen Lloyd for his part in rescuing thirteen men from the *Kenilworth* that had struck rocks on its way from New Orleans carrying cotton and tobacco. In 1965 an inshore lifeboat station was established in Abersoch with a D-Class lifeboat and a new boathouse to house the trolley and tractor needed for launching. A new Atlantic 85 boat named *Peter and Ann Setten* arrived in 2015 funded by the bequest of Ann Setten of Shropshire. The most recent bravery award was presented to four crew members in September 2001 for the rescue of a young girl and her dog trapped on rocks at Porth Ceiriad.

The nature of the callouts now

left: Granite Quarry;
right: Abersoch Boat Yard

reflect the changes in sea traffic and the character of Abersoch. In the past the vast majority of 'shouts' involved shipping in trouble whereas nowadays speedboats, jet skis, paddle boarders and swimmers account for most of the emergencies.

By the 1950s, a way for a family to raise an income was for them to move into a shed or caravan for a few months and let out the house to visitors.

Further south at **Penrhyn Du** are a number of lead mines. By the turn of

above: *Penrhyn Du; left: Penrhyn Mill; right: St Engan's Church*

the 20th century mining had ceased, the last recorded output being five tons in 1930. Here are the remains of an 18th century Cornish engine house that contained a steam engine to pump water from the lead mine, probably built by the Cornish miners who came here to work.

Going west to **Llanengan** is St Engan's Church that originally dates to the 13th century. During the later

Middle Ages it became an important pilgrimage site, housing the shrine of St Engan a late 5th century ruler of Llŷn. Engan gifted Bardsey to Cadfan and the island is visible from the churchyard.

By the door is an ancient wooden chest carved from a single piece of wood that originally had three locks with the keys given to the vicar and two church wardens.

Porth Neigwl (Hell's Mouth) stretches for nearly four miles from

Mynydd Cilan to Mynydd Rhiw. The aptly named Hell's Mouth was dangerous to sailing ships due to the strong prevailing southwesterly wind that drove ships into the bay from where they had little chance of escape. Captains would often try and ground the ship onto the beach with the hope that they could be refloated in calmer weather but most broke up on impact. There is thought to have been at least

left: Porth Neigwl; top right: Stone Age axe factory; below: St Aeirhiw's Church

140 shipwrecks over the last 200 years in the bay.

Round the coast and overlooking Porth Neigwl is **Y Rhiw** a small village built on the side of Mynydd Rhiw. From the village there are fantastic views right along the beach far below. To the northeast of the summit is an area strewn with stones thought to be the remains of a Stone Age axe factory.

St Aeirhiw's Church was built in 1860 on the footings of an earlier church. The churchyard contains the

above: Plas yn Rhiw; top right: Porth Neigwl; below: Mynydd y Graig

graves of the many bodies that were washed up at Porth Neigwl during the First World War. I have been told that R. S. Thomas who was the vicar in the 1960's refused to hold services here as he felt it was inhabited by an evil spirit!

At the bottom of Mynydd Rhiw is Plas yn Rhiw, a manor house owned by the National Trust. It was built in the 17th century for John Lewis (not of the shop fame), whose family descended from a 9th century king of Powys who had resided at Rhiw since Tudor times.

Manganese was discovered in 1827 and donkeys carried the ore down to Porth Neigwl. The industry became a substantial employer in the village and 200 people were employed in 1906. By 1914, due to the vast amount of rock that needed to be removed for shipping, an aerial ropeway was constructed that took the ore over the village down to a jetty on the shore.

Mynydd y Graig looks like a great

fortress of massive boulders that dominates Y Rhiw skyline facing towards the sea with fantastic panoramic views from the cliff top looking over to Mynydd Penarfynydd and Porth Neigwl. There are three hillforts and several hut circles here thought to be Iron Age and a Bronze Age cinerary urn was found nearby in 1955.

Further west near the coast at **Llanfaelrhys** is a classically simple, single-chamber church dedicated to St

Maelrhys who was a 7th century missionary and Cadfan's cousin. It is open most of the year during daylight hours and one of only two locations on the Llŷn where Bardsey can be seen from the churchyard. Passing through a narrow, low Norman doorway there are simple rustic benches on the north side and box pews on the south with an early medieval font placed at the west end. On the wall is a beautiful piece of embroidery of the southern pilgrimage route along Llŷn Peninsular by Mabel Leigh that was gifted to the church by her family after her death.

Up a tiny staircase is '*Llofft R. S. Thomas*' a tribute room to R. S. Thomas who was vicar here from 1967 to 1978. It is set out with pictures, books and CDs and is a quiet sanctuary where one can sit and read or listen to music associated with Thomas' work.

On the Coastal Path at **Ysgo**, mining for manganese began in 1827 at and was originally carried by donkey to Porth Cadlan for loading onto small sailing ships. In the late 1800s it became one of the largest manganese mines in North Wales and in 1904 a steep tramway was built down to Porth Ysgo beach with the wagons controlled by cables attached to a set of winding houses. Porth Ysgo jetty was last used in 1927 and manganese mining ceased here in 1945.

According to Welsh legend, Gwaith Camlan (the Battle of Camlan), is

left: St Maelrhys' Church;
right: Manganese Quarry wheels

where Arthur's final fight with Mordred took place in 537, either on the small beach at Porth Cadlan or more likely on the field above. After the battle, Arthur's mortally wounded body was taken by boat by three women for burial on Bardsey (the legendary Afallon – *Avalon*). Mordred perished but Arthur's army is said to have triumphed in the end. Legend says that the battle was started when a knight drew his sword against orders to kill a

left: Manganese Quarry; right: Porth Cadlan

snake; unsheathing a sword broke the rules of the truce.

Maen Gwenonwy (*Gwenonwy's rock*) is a small offshore island with a causeway joined to Porth Cadlan at low tide, and is said to be named in memory of King Arthur's sister. She married Gwyndaf Hen whose remains are buried on Bardsey and their son Hywyn became the patron saint of the church at Aberdaron.

Inland at **Rhoshirwaun** is Canolfan Felin Uchaf. Set up in 2004, a group of friends raised funds to purchase the old farm for development as a centre for living arts and science. It has since grown to become one of the most celebrated environmental and cultural initiatives in Wales. Small businesses based at the Green Enterprise Centre provide opportunities for students to work alongside experienced craftspeople who offer apprentiships in specific craft and land-based skills.

above: Pink Campion and Wild Garlic; right: Felin Uchaf

Aberdaron to Bardsey Island / Ynys Enlli

The shoreline here is part of the Aberdaron Coast and Bardsey Island Special Protection Area and was designated a Heritage Coast in 1974. Pen Llŷn a'r Sarnau Special Area of Conservation, is one of the largest marine sites in the UK. Daron (from which Aberdaron gets its name) was the ancient Celtic goddess of oak trees.

The coast around Aberdaron has been the place of many shipwrecks. In 1752 the schooner John the Baptist was wrecked on the beach and in 1822 the Bardsey lighthouse tender sank with the loss of six lives.

below: Map of Shipwrecks; right: St Hywyn's Church

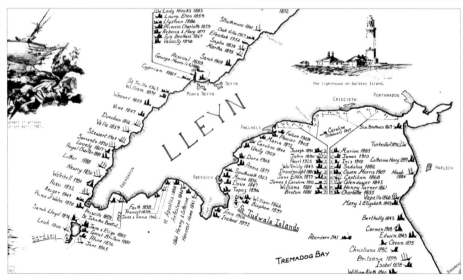

The stretch of water between the main land and Bardsey called Swnt Enlli/Bardsey Sound is notorious for its tidal race. It is especially dangerous when a spring tide is running coupled with a strong easterly wind. Many ships have been wrecked here over the years including the Schooner Voelas lost in the Sound in 1869 in dense fog and mainly due to this shipwreck, a foghorn was installed in the lighthouse on Bardsey in 1878.

Aberdaron was the haunt of smugglers, a common occurrence in small seaside villages in times gone by often driven by poverty and hardship. The remote coves and caves were ideal for concealment and Aberdaron was within reach of the main contraband coasts of the Isle of Man and Ireland. Loot from the wrecks was an added bonus and it was difficult for customs officials to police the rugged coastline

below: Aberdaron shoreline;
top right: Prayer mats;
below: Early gravestones St Hywyn's Church

(and local officials were often the smugglers' customers!) Smuggling was not considered a crime until 1536 when it was made a capital offence.

The origins of the church date from 5th to 7th when it was founded by **St Hywyn**, an early Welsh saint and St Cadfan's cousin and steward. It became the parish church in the 12th century when Bardsey Island was declared a place of pilgrimage by the Papacy, the church became a significant pilgrimage site throughout

In memory of the crew of
MV SWANLAND
Captain Yury Shmelev
Chief Officer Leonid Safonov
Chief Engineer Gennady Meshkov
2nd Engineer Mikhail Starchevoy
Able Seaman Sergey Kharchenko
Cook Oleg Andriets

Lost off Bardsey Island
whilst on passage from
Llanddulas to Cowes
27th November 2011

That those who are safe on land may
ever remember and pray for the many
who go down to the sea in ships

the Middle Ages. Both the north and southern Llŷn pilgrimage routes meet here because of its importance as an embarkation point for the abbey on Bardsey.

St Hywyn held the ancient privilege of sanctuary. Near the altar stood a stone chair from which no fugitive could lawfully be ejected by his enemy. In 1115, Gruffudd ap Rhys took refuge here to escape being handed over to Henry 1 of England who had invaded Gwynedd the previous year. The soldiers tried to take the ex-prince by force but were beaten back by the clergy. Following the conquest of Gwynedd by Edward 1 in 1284, he held court in Nefyn and visited Aberdaron on his way to St Mary's Abbey on Bardsey.

Two carved stones displayed against the northeast wall are possibly the gravestones of two early priests, Versacius and Senacus, who were

left: M V Swanland gravestone;
right: Jasper Stone sea defence

members of a local small religious community. The stones are natural boulders and the clear lettering and inscriptions are thought to be late 5th or early 6th century.

In the churchyard, there are several memorials marking the resting place of sea captains and sailors. One gravestone mentions the names of six Russian crew members of M V Swanland lost off Bardsey carrying limestone in a gale-force storm enroute to Cowes on 27 November 2011.

The poet R. S. Thomas was vicar of Aberdaron from 1967 to 1978. Born in Cardiff, son of a ship's captain, he was ordained in 1936. The surrounding landscape was of endless poetic inspiration for him and he continued to live nearby after his retirement. The church is a setting for his poetry; he writes:

> "...in cities that
> have outgrown their promise people
> are becoming pilgrims
> again, if not to this place,
> then to the recreation of it
> in their own spirits..."

Jasper, a red aggregate quartz stone was mined nearby at **Llanllawen**; Aberdaron beach is strewn with pieces of all sizes including huge ones that are part of the sea defenses. Particularly popular for making jewellery, the stone has been used as a carving material for thousands of years.

Pilgrimages to Bardsey ended sometime in the 16th century but resumed in the 21st. The new pilgrims may not share the religious fervor of the early monks but there is a real sense of tranquility to be found here. St Hywyn's feature music, poetry, meditation and prayer in their worship schedule for pilgrims and visitors to Aberdaron.

Where Afon Saint meets Bae Aberdaron at Porth-y-Simdde, is the remains of a jetty running into the sea. Built in the 19th century, it was used for exporting heavy crystal ore from workings at Gwaith Pompren. There is also what is left of an old building

left: Porth-y-Simdde; right: Porth Meudwy

nearby that was probably a corn grinding mill. This small cove is accessible by a set of steep steps and is cut off at high tide.

Porth Meudwy (meudwy: *hermit*), a small fishing port, was the traditional embarkation point for pilgrims crossing the Sound to Bardsey. During bad weather the island could be cut off for weeks and pilgrims would need to wait in Aberdaron. Today this little cove still serves as the departure point, and Colin the Boatman takes over everything needed for the island including residents, modern pilgrims, day visitors, bird-watchers, cattle, sheep and the post. A handful of local fishermen keep their boats, nets, tractors and lobster pots here and make a living catching crab and lobster in the waters around Aberdaron.

In October 1917 Porth Meudwy became the arrival point for seven sailors who had survived the sinking of their steamship by a German submarine the previous week. They were weakened by hunger when they

made landfall in their lifeboat and received hot food and dry clothes from local residents. They then went by bus to Pwllheli and eventually headed for Liverpool.

Ffynnon Fair (*St Mary's well*) is a natural spring near the foot of the cliff of Mynydd Mawr. The way down to it is treacherous especially when wet as I know from experience! The steps (known as Grisiau Mair) are cut into

left: Old winch;
right: Ffynnon Fair and Grisiau Mair

the rock and are steep and worn away to gravel in places by the feet of thousands of pilgrims over hundreds of years scrambling down to take a drink. The well was famed for its healing powers and purity, and is not contaminated by seawater being ten feet above high water (according to latest research findings). The well has been immortalized by R. S. Thomas in his poem 'Ffynnon Fair'.

Joan Abbott Parry, sixteen year-old daughter of a Manchester judge,

drowned here in 1904. She was standing on the rocks very near the sea when a large wave carried her away and her body was not recovered for several days – she is buried in Aberdaron churchyard.

The foundations and outline of Capel Mair, the medieval pilgrim church of St Mary, can still be seen on the grass slope of Braich y Pwll and was the last in a string of pilgrimage chapels on the way to Bardsey. Here pilgrims would offer prayers for a safe journey across the dangerous Sound. Sailors and fishermen would pray here to ask for protection from the perils of the hazardous crossing.

On the rocky headland is Maen Melyn Llŷn, a huge rock that looks like a creature turned to stone. According to the National Trust Interpretation Board nearby, it was placed here in the Bronze Age and later used by pilgrims as the final marker at the end of the Llŷn before the crossing.

left: Maen Melyn Llŷn;
right: Swnt Enlli (Bardsey Sound)

Bardsey / Ynys Enlli

"In Welsh, ynys yn y llif, island in the flood-tide, in English, or rather Norse, Bardr's Island, the place has been lived on almost continuously through recorded history, and visited, at least, for thousands of years before that, as worked flints from the Mesolithic and Bronze Age cremations testify. It's a fragment of land at the edge, first landfall after the Irish Sea."

Christine Evans – '*Bardsey*'

I have made the five mile boat journey from Porth Meudwy over to **Bardsey** many times, sometimes in quite rough weather, but have always felt completely safe with Colin in his yellow boat. As I sit watching the passing waves I think of those early pilgrims facing this perilous journey that would have taken much longer in a small sailing boat! I wonder at the religious zeal that must have inspired them to brave this crossing to reach their 'promised land'.

Hut circles and other evidence such as stones chipped and sharpened into tools and worked flints found in various places on the island confirm that people have lived here at least since Neolithic time, well before it became a focus for the early Celtic Christians.

The original monks lived in individual cells with a larger building for eating and communal prayer. Marks

of a field system with small round huts enclosed within a boundary wall are visible above Ty Pellaf and were possibly the earliest Christian settlement on the island.

By the 5th century Bardsey was known as the *'island of the saints'* and Einion Frenin, Prince of Llŷn, invited Cadfan to found a clas on the island. He arrived in the 6th century with 25

The Cadfan Way – A Journey from Tywyn to Bardsey

kinsmen and become the first head of the religious settlement. The settlement came to be named St Mary's Abbey in the 11th century.

In the 12th century Pope Calixtus 11 declared that three pilgrimages to Bardsey equaled one to Rome and soon growing numbers of pilgrims were gathering in Aberdaron, sleeping in St Hywyn's Church and cooking their meals at Y Gegin Fawr. Bardsey is known as '*the island of 20,000 saint, martyrs and confessors*'; the word '*saint*'

simply signified a person of devout faith. Pilgrims believed that dying on Bardsey would save them from the fires of eternal damnation and they would ascend directly to heaven, and that internment in its soil would bestow sainthood upon them. Medieval bards called Bardsey '*the land of indulgences, absolution and pardons, the road to heaven and the gate to Paradise*'. Monks were paid to carry embalmed corpses from church to church along the Llŷn pilgrim routes for burial on Bardsey

and '*coffin ships*' sailed out of Barmouth, Abererch and Caernarfon bringing more bodies for burial on the island.

Human bones are occasionally still being found at the north end of the island and Christine Evans (writer, poet and long-time resident) told me she has seen skulls piled at the side of a trench dug in the 1970s. They were yellowed, strong-jawed with extremely ground-down teeth. Bones found are buried with reverence near the chapel.

In medieval times the island was a major centre of pilgrimage and in 1212 belonged to the Augustinian Canons Regular. Edward 1 visited in 1284 and special permission was required to enable Queen Eleanor and two ladies-in-waiting to accompany the King as no women were allowed on the island at that time. Twenty shiploads of servants and notables are recorded as staying in tents and treasury accounts show payments for '25 *tentmen and 4 carpenters*'. On the strength of the

revenue from this visit the Abbey was able to build the tower, the remains of which can be seen today.

Because of Henry VIII, the monastery was dissolved and its buildings demolished in 1537 but the island remains a spiritual destination for pilgrims to this day.

2016 was the 1,500th anniversary of St Cadfan setting up his clas in Tywyn, Meirionnydd. As part of a diocean pilgrimage project, the Diocese of Bangor are compiling a new pilgrimage route to be named The Cadfan Way starting from St Cadfan's Church in Tywyn and finishing on Bardsey Island. The Diocese are providing a platform for poets, musicians and historians to explore ancient churches and locations along the route and the project will reach its peak at the Eifionydd National Eisteddfod in 2023 being held in Boduan near Pwllheli. The Cadfan Way mainly follows the coast and it is hoped to establish it as a popular pilgrimage for the future.

Bardsey is recognized both nationally and internationally important for wildlife and is a National Nature Reserve and SSSI and safeguarded by many other environmental and conservation protection orders and long may it continue to be so! Its unique position attracts migrant birds and is one of the most important staging posts for birds in the Irish Sea.

As soon as I set foot on Bardsey I feel a sense of stillness settle over me.

"*Bardsey Now and Then*", a recent book of mine, contains a diary I wrote while on a residency here and is full of images and my thoughts about this beautiful place and it also contains two diaries of previous inhabitants, one from the late 1800s and another from the 1920s.

The absolute wonder of being here; whether sitting watching the seals' antics at Yr Honllwyn, hearing the choughs calling overhead or listening to the shrill cries of Manx Shearwaters

as they fly in from the sea at night, are just a small part of what makes the island such a unique and special place and I will continue to return to this magical island, my spiritual home, as long as I am able to do so. Words written in a short verse, *englyn* in Welsh, by J. Glyn Davies and often quoted by a dear friend of mine (Twm Elias) say it all:

"Lle i enaid gael llonydd"
"Where a soul may find peace."

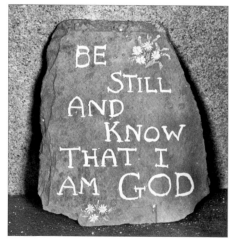

Acknowledgements

It would have been impossible to write this book about the history of this part of northwest Wales without a great deal of help and advice from many organisations, charities and individual people.

I have listed below those I would like to thank for their assistance in accompanying me on this epic journey, help in research, telling me their intriguing stories and free 'hotel' accommodation!

Debbie Ashton
Ken Bridges
Chris and Dave Bursnall
Myrddin ap Dafydd
Dave Davis
K Carroll
Gill Caves
Berni Cavanagh
Hilary Dent
Twm Elias
Dewi Evans
Nick Evans
Sue Fogarty
Heather Garrett
Meryl Gover
Annie Grundy
Rev Ruth Hansford
Geoff Hill
Annie and Phil Horsley
Shelagh Hourahane
Sara Hulls
Suzanne Iuppa
Pete Jarrad
Grif Jones
Stephen K Land
Valerie Land
Jane Lloyd Frances
Samantha, Dave & Joe MacCall
John McEllhenney
Jenny McGugan
Robert Owen
Ben and Jo Porter
Vanessa Priestley
Gill Ray
Alun John Richards
Hefin and Meirion Richards
Andrew Smallbone
Angela & Bill Swann
Dianna Tregenza
Meri Wells
Jane Whittle
Claire Williams
Gwenfair Williams
Sue and Aled Williams
Jan Woods
Ysgol Penybryn

A huge thank you to Steve Porter for permission use his image of Bardsey from the air taken when paragliding!

A special thanks to Christine Evans whose knowledge of the history of Bardsey/Ynys Enlli and the saints is unsurpassed, to Carole Shearman for her excellent editing of my Introduction and especially to Kate Coldham who yet again has turned my amateur writing into something worthy of publishing.

Useful Organisations/Websites

Bardsey Island Trust
Bywyd Gwyllt Glaslyn Wildlife
Cadw
Coflein – catalogue of archaeological sites
Diocese of Bangor
Ffestiniog & Welsh Highland Railways
Gwasg Carreg Gwalch
Gwynedd Archaeological Trust
Historic Wales

Llanfair Slate Caverns
Natural Resources Wales
National Trust Wales
North Wales Wildlife Trust
Ordnance Survey Maps
Porthmadog Marine Museum
RSPB
Wales Coastal Path
Wales Tourist Board

Works Consulted

A Guide to Ancient & Historic Wales – Frances Lynch

A Llŷn Anthology – Dewi Roberts

A Tale of Two Rivers – The Dyfi and Mawddach – Alun Richards & Jean Napier

Bardsey – Christine Evans

Bardsey Now and Then – Jean Napier

Cadfan's Church – Meryl Gover

Celtic Britain – Homer Sykes

Circular Walks in Meirionnydd – Dorothy Hamilton

Gerald of Wales – The Journey Through Wales Trans: Lewis Thorpe

Holy Ways of Wales – Jim Green

Land of Sacred Legends – Graham Murphy

Llŷn – Elfed Gruffydd

Llŷn The Peninsular's Story – Michael Senior

Llŷn – The peninsular and its past explored – Ioan Roberts

Meini Meirionnydd – Huw Dylan Owen

On Track – Suzanne Iuppa

Pilgrimage A Welsh Perspective – Terry John & Nona Rees

Real Gwynedd – Rhys Mwyn

Rhinogydd Ancient Routes and Old Roads – Jean Napier

The Ancient Wells of Llŷn – Roland Bond

The Cambrian Coast – Pwllheli to Harlech – Editor: Ioan Roberts

The Celtic Year – Shirley Toulson

The Church of St Celynnin Llangelynnin – Stephen K Land

The Mawddach Ardudwy Trail – David Berry

The Settlements of the Celtic Saints – E G Bowen

The Snowdonia National Park – W M Condry

The Standing Stones of North-Western Wales – Michael Senior

Two Snowdonia Rivers – Alun Richards & Jean Napier

Wales A History – Wynford Vaughan-Thomas

Wales Coastal Path Llŷn Peninsular – Carl Rogers & Tony Bowerman

Walks around the Ancient Churches of Llŷn – Christopher Nichols

Walks around Barmouth and the Mawddach Estuary – David Berry

Walks on the Llŷn Peninsular Part 1 South & West – N Burras & J Stiff

Welcome to Harlech-Bermo – Owain Maredudd

COMPACT CYMRU

– MORE TITLES;

FULL OF COLOUR IMAGES
AND CONCISE WRITING

www.carreg-gwalch.cymru

Jean Napier

Bardsey
Now and Then

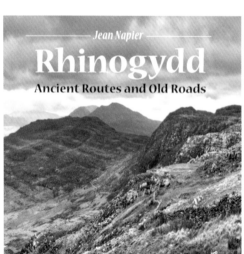

Jean Napier

Rhinogydd
Ancient Routes and Old Roads

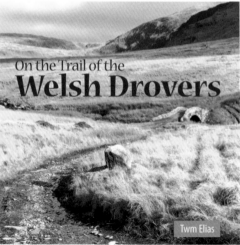

On the Trail of the
Welsh Drovers

Twm Elias